BRIDGES OF FAITH

BRIDGES of FAITH

Building a Relationship With a Sister Parish

DENNIS P. O'CONNOR

A PERSONAL JOURNAL

ST. ANTHONY MESSENGER PRESS

Cincinnati, Ohio

"Ten Commandments for Mission Trip Participants" and "Five Tips for Safe Travel" by Howard Culbertson from www.ShortTermMissions.com are reprinted with permission of the author.

Cover design by Mark Sullivan
Book design by Jennifer Tibbits

LIBRARY OF CONGRESS CATALOGING-IN-PUBLICATION DATA

O'Connor, Dennis P.
Bridges of faith : a personal journal / Dennis P. O'Connor.
p. cm.
Includes index.
ISBN 978-0-86716-794-8 (pbk. : alk. paper) 1. Catholic Church—Missions. 2. Church work with the poor—Catholic Church. 3. Church and social problems—Catholic Church. 4. Faith-based human services. I. Title.

BV2190.O265 2007
266'.2—dc22

2007038867

ISBN: 978-0-86716-794-8

Published by St. Anthony Messenger Press
28 W. Liberty St.
Cincinnati, OH 45202
www.AmericanCatholic.org

Printed in the United States of America.

Printed on acid-free paper.

07 08 09 10 11 5 4 3 2 1

"Twinning partnerships are beautiful relationships of faith. These partnerships become opportunities for both sides to share life, love, faith and prayer together. Good twinning relationships that work are wonderful to witness."

—Oscar Cardinal Rodriguez of Honduras

"A day never passes that I don't spend a significant amount of time pondering the experiences of my trip. Each of these interludes ends with the same question: "What am I supposed to do with this?" In the meantime, I listen, I learn, wait for God's nudge…and take Spanish lessons!"

—Kathy Born, El Salvador delegation member

CONTENTS

Faith-Based Partnerships Defined

"At a time of dramatic global changes and challenges, Catholics in the United States face special responsibilities and opportunities. We are members of a universal church that transcends national boundaries and calls us to live in solidarity and justice with the peoples of the world. We are also citizens of a powerful democracy with enormous influence beyond our borders. As (Christians) and Americans, we are uniquely called to global solidarity."[1]

    —from *Called to Global Solidarity: International Challenges for United States Parishes.*

Introduction

IT was because of this call made by the United States Roman Catholic Bishops in 1997 that much of today's parish twinning or "sister parish" projects have blossomed in North America. Nurtured in a decentralized fashion across the continent, faith communities from every corner of the wealthiest land history has known have been reaching out across borders and oceans to extend helping hands and bridges of hope and faith to their brothers and sisters.

In that environment was born the *Bridges of Faith* project. This booklet is a partner piece to the manual *Bridges of Faith*, a book designed to present "best practices" and anecdotal accounts of dozens of past and current twinning programs throughout North America. It serves as an initial source book and idea book for members of churches, schools and other faith communities to help set up their own faith-based partnerships. *Bridges of Faith* not only highlights the journey of faith that many faith communities have embarked upon but also offers detailed accounts of how they proceeded with their partnerships. It provides detailed accounts of how parishioners became involved in their partnerships, how the covenants were initiated and what those involved in the twinning relationships experienced.

This booklet is a hands-on workbook meant for individual members of a faith community's twinning team, the active participants who will be engaged in the "bridge building" at your parish or church. Most often, participants using this personal journal will be those making trips to the twinning partners' home, whether that be in a remote corner of the United States or in a foreign land. But it also can be used by friends or family members who, although not making the journey, want to keep track of the partnership for themselves. *Bridges of Faith: A Personal Journal* also can be given to twinning partners, mirroring their experiences with your own,

using the booklet as a tool for everyone to remember those important shared experiences.

As Reverend Joe Bragotti, a Comboni missionary now based in Guatemala, advises those embarking on faith-based partnerships of any kind, "before you go, have in mind what it is that you will do when you return."

This workbook is structured to walk you through the steps of discovering why you are going, where you are going, what to do when you are "on the ground" with your twinning partner, and what you will do when you return. The workbook has been designed for you to take notes, paste photos and staple memos inside. It is a tool to help you record important milestones in the establishment of your faith-based partnership, and it easily can be used in conjunction with the journal you will keep from your journey.

There is no right way or wrong way to go about keeping track of your journey. But I have learned from numerous twinning trips, short-term immersion encounters and even informational press visits to the Holy Land and other destinations, that if I write the important things down as they happen or while I'm thinking about them—who I've met, where I've been, what conversations were about—my ability to recollect (and therefore my ability to describe these journeys to others) is all that much easier. This should serve as an important way for you to retain and share those memories.

And so, good luck and God bless you on this very special journey, a journey of social justice and solidarity.

—Dennis P. O'Connor

What Am I Doing Here?

After a lot of prayer and consideration, you finally have made the decision to join your school or faith community's twinning project. So, you might ask, just what am I doing here? What have I gotten myself into? What can I expect to discover through this process? Who will I meet? Just how do I get the ball rolling? To what new avenues of faith and justice could this take me?

All good questions.

First, let's look at the parameters of your church's faith-based partnership. The twinning relationship or sister-parish partnership you are engaged upon is rooted in faith and must by its very nature be a joyous adventure in faith, a partnership that is ongoing, active and mutually shared. It is defined by the written commitment your church and your twinning partner have agreed upon. If you are joining a partnership that already is under way, you have heard the stories about the deep friendships that have been developed by your parish and your faith partners overseas (or wherever they may be…even just down the road).

If your faith-based partnership is just getting started, then you will discover that you'll begin by developing these new friendships yourself, forging relationships that will be defined by a mutual concern about both communities and their individual members. You will, together, define what your covenant of hope and faith will be and how you will carry that out.

It is here that we borrow from our great depth and wealth of history as a missionary people: We are all hoping to work in solidarity to help create the kingdom of justice and peace together. We will share the gospel message with each other, providing a translation of what its meaning is to us and our partners, hoping to better understand who each of us is and what we can become.

The *Sister Parish Handbook* by the SHARE Foundation, a California-based partnership facilitator, explains that twinning is built on developing relationships. "It is people of two different cultural backgrounds sharing their faith, their similarities and their uniqueness. It is a relationship in which both communities become more aware of their call to experience the face of Jesus in all people, regardless of language, culture, economic status, and ethnicity. It truly becomes an immersion, conversion, and an empowering experience."

QUESTIONS FOR REFLECTION

1. Why have I joined my faith community's twinning project?

2. What are my personal expectations?

3. What expectations do I have for the group?

4. What experiences do I have that are comparable to joining this faith-based partnership?

5. Can I apply any of those experiences to this journey?

6. What are my biggest concerns about embarking on this journey of faith?

7. What do I look forward to most?

8. What skills do I have that I believe will be of benefit to the overall partnership's endeavor?

9. How can these gifts be applied in this partnership?

10. What kind of commitment am I willing to make in this partnership?

Seven Reasons to Establish Faith-based Partnerships

According to the Mission Office of the Archdiocese of Cincinnati, there are seven reasons to establish faith-based partnerships. They are:

- Faith-based partnerships make us realize that we belong to a universal church that is invited and commanded by Jesus to work and pray for the unity and solidarity of all humankind. We are all members of one family of God recognizing the presence of Christ in all.
- Faith-based partnerships show us that our own church community, our understanding of the Bible and God and our personal faith development are deeply enriched when we discover the various ways the Holy Spirit inspires various cultures around the United States and the world.
- Faith-based partnerships promote mutuality, respect and peace in our families, society and world. Just as a healthy friendship and marriage bring out the best of both partners, so does twinning.
- Faith-based partnerships are a commitment to not having a mission, but being the mission of Jesus in order to expand the self-identity of a parish, to create larger consciousnesses and bigger, more compassionate hearts.
- Faith-based partnerships invite a Vatican II understanding and ecclesiology of church where ordinary laypeople on both sides of the twinning relationship take on their own responsibility to develop leadership, outreach and empowerment.
- Faith-based partnerships help to eliminate the grave sins of racism, sexism, militarism, paternalism, materialism, imperialism, class-superiority and xenophobia as ordinary people learn and appreciate each other's cultures and spirituality through mutual respect and sharing of gifts, talents and resources within the body of Christ.
- Faith-based partnerships encourage a hunger for Catholic social teaching to study and solve the deeper causes of poverty, hunger and exploitation locally and globally. Faith-based partnerships invite a move away from models of dependency and charity to models of social justice and empowerment.

What Is a Faith-based Partnership?

Whether called twinning or a sister-parish relationship, a faith-based partnership is a journey of solidarity between peoples of multiple faith communities, often in different countries. More often than not, faith partners abroad face numerous obstacles that we in North America would find staggering: Hunger, poverty, violence and a sense of being dispossessed all frame the parameters of life in most of the rest of the world.

Throughout North America, one can find thousands of examples of Christian communities reaching out to build bridges of faith and hope to their brothers and sisters throughout the world—particularly with our neighbors in Central and South America, from where so many new immigrants are arriving into the United States nearly every day in search of a better life; and increasingly with the poor in Africa and Asia, where a renewed commitment to those in need there has energized the Western world.

"When a parish or diocese in the United States has a relationship with a parish or diocese in another country, it can be an opportunity for growth, friendship and faith-development for all the people involved," said Susan Thompson, from the Columban Peace and Justice Office in an address at Mission Congress 2000. "It is an opportunity for understanding the religious, economic and political realities of a group of people with whom we have entered into relationships. It can be through short-term mission experiences that an understanding of belonging to something much bigger than ourselves, our own parish, or even the United States church grows. We begin to understand that it is not just 'my relationship' with my family, my parishioners, or even my own community that is important; but, as I understand that I am connected to my brothers and sisters in the whole world, I have to rethink my choices, my country's policies, and my own lifestyle as they affect the lives of those with whom I am now in relationship."

The need for building bridges of hope and faith seems obvious. And thousands of Christians throughout North America have taken the challenge issued by the bishops and the church to heart, not only reaching out to their new neighbors who have come to North America, but also visiting their homelands, establishing friendships, agreeing to covenants of faith and commitments to solidarity and prayer for each other in order to transform lives and unjust social structures.

Put succinctly, a faith-based partnership is the act of imitating Christ as he reaches out to his flock, offering comfort, a smile, solidarity, friendship and sometimes tangible kinds of help that we are able to provide. It is being engaged in a mutually enriching spirituality and social justice. And it is recognizing that our commonality—our shared humanity—transcends all borders, ethnicities and economic divergence.

A Model for the Twinning Relationship

If there is a model to emulate in the twinning relationship, it might best be compared to the marriage relationship or a deep friendship, according to Mike Gable, a former Maryknoll lay missioner and now director of the Mission Office at the Archdiocese of Cincinnati.

If you enter into a relationship because you feel sorry for someone, that relationship is most likely doomed to failure. The attributes of a good marriage or deep friendship include trust, respect, mutuality, solidarity, participation, a shared-faith in Christ and good communication. It is a relationship based on love.

In that same vein, if you come into the partnership thinking that the United States is the best place in the world and nobody can match us, especially a poor twinning partner living in a developing country, you very likely will be disappointed in the long run. A faith-based partnership based on pity, money, American chauvinism, paternalism and an attitude that "we have all the answers" quickly can lead to mistrust and a failed endeavor.

The image you have in mind about your faith-based partnership reflects how your twinning relationship probably will evolve. In the sometimes confusing era of a post-9/11 world, it might be wise to revisit important documents that explore establishing faith-based partnerships, especially the United States Bishops' 1997 document, *Called to Global Solidarity: International Challenges for U.S. Parishes.* It defines solidarity as the foundational block of faith partnerships, giving you a sound basis for establishing your twinning relationship on the front end of the process.

QUESTIONS FOR REFLECTION

1. Describe a friendship you have and cherish. What are the attributes of that friendship that make it work?

2. How might you apply those same attributes with your partners in a twinning relationship?

"Heroic" Versus "Humble" Partnerships

In the training material developed by the Mission Office of the Archdiocese of Cincinnati for faith-based partnerships, there are two basic models widely recognized in mission circles that encompass the "style" of partnerships that are often witnessed throughout the developing world. Described as either "heroic" or "humble" models of interaction, the descriptions below are self-explanatory. For our purposes in building bridges of hope and faith, we support the "humble" model.

"HEROIC MODEL" BASED ON CHARITY AND DEPENDENCY

Motivations: Why am I involved in this process?
To engage in a process of "fixing" a problem, to help "them" change and become more like me. I am motivated out of a sense of paternalism and pity for their situation. If these people were more like us, we could help them alleviate more of their problems and make the world a better place.

Qualities/characteristics/values/attitudes:
I have a duty to help out, showing these people the best way of doing things.

Goals and purposes:
I will provide my expertise and help these people build a better world by living the way I do, and by doing things the way I do.

Objectives—what to achieve by when:
I have a clear timetable, a business plan, that needs to be in place. I will check back often to make sure my plan is being carried out according to my calendar.

Strategies—concrete ways to achieve goals and objectives:
My way is the best way to get things done. We have shown in the United States that we have the best solutions for achieving goals, and we will apply those techniques here. We have money to give out to these poor people, but there are going to be strings attached to how that money is used. Refer back to my business plan, as stated above.

Participants:
We are the elite of our group, the experts in our community. If you have any questions, please check our resumes.

"HUMBLE MODEL" BASED ON SOLIDARITY AND MUTUALITY

Motivations: Why am I involved in this process?
I'm responding to Jesus' call for unity and love for humanity, to build up the body of Christ and to be part of the growth of God's kingdom. I want to enrich and expand my personal faith development as well as the church's growth. I want to empower lay leadership among both partners in the spirit of Vatican II. I recognize that both parties can benefit and learn from unique gifts that can be spiritual, theological, ecclesiastical, social, and consisting of talents, skills, prayer, song, services and material.

Qualities/characteristics/values/attitudes:
I will act with humility, flexibility, open-mindedness, and engage in dialogue.

Goals and purposes:
I want to become more catholic (universal) in my thoughts, words and actions. I seek to change personal lifestyles and power structures for the common good. I hope to build and further community in both faith communities.

Objectives—what to achieve by when:
Through dialogue and agreement, our faith communities will establish covenants and deadlines for whatever we agree shall be done mutually. It is better to take the long view and make sure that everyone is in agreement.

Strategies, concrete ways to achieve goals and objectives:
I will refer to the tenets of Catholic Social Teaching to help guide me in this partnership. I will foster ongoing formation of both partners

in the study of social, economic, political, and religious issues with our partners. I will help foster reciprocal visits with our partners, and I will be part of the effort to enact communications with them.

Participants:

We are part of a wide spectrum of people within our faith community, including youths, parish council, pastor, the school, RCIA, liturgy commission and any other groups that might have an interest and stake in the partnership.

Catholic Social Teaching and Faith-based Partnerships

Among the many meditations faith communities can engage in prior to becoming involved in a twinning relationship abroad is to consider the key elements of Catholic social teaching (see list on p. 13)—filled with concise statements about how the church views the constructive building of a society based upon many years of reflection. These points provide an excellent framework within which to construct your bridges of hope and faith.

The United States Catholic Bishops define the importance of Catholic Social Teaching in a reflection titled "Sharing Catholic Social Teaching: Challenges and Directions," excerpted below:

> Catholic Social Teaching emerges from the truth of what God has revealed to us about himself. We believe in the triune God whose very nature is communal and social. God the Father sends his only Son Jesus Christ and shares the Holy Spirit as his gift of love. God reveals himself to us as one who is not alone, but rather as one who is relational, one who is Trinity. Therefore, we who are made in God's image share this communal, social nature. We are called to reach out and to build relationships of love and justice.
>
> Catholic Social Teaching is based on and inseparable from our understanding of human life and human dignity. Every human being is created in the image of God

Why You Should *Not* Embark on a Twinning Trip

David Armstrong from www.ShortTermMissions.org states that there are "Seven Reasons Why You Should Never Go On a Short-term Mission Trip." With his permission, I have summarized and embellished his tongue-in-cheek "warnings" below.

Warning!
Embarking on a short term mission will:

- Distort your perception of the world. Seeing the world through the plastic lenses of our society is sufficient. Once you have traveled the globe, your views may be become distorted. *Don't needlessly mess yourself up.*
- Get you sick or you could get robbed. It's dangerous out there. Some places have a crime rate almost as high as *our* inner cities.
- Make you harder to live with. The way you view life and even your likes and dislikes are liable to change. Your friends and family probably won't understand or appreciate your sudden changes.

- Make you feel awkward at some of the jokes and comments you currently enjoy. Racist or insensitive jokes will not seem as funny when you have seen life from the other side.
- Experience sadness you haven't felt before. After you see real suffering, you won't pay much attention to your complaining about how hard you've got it. You are even liable to feel guilty and uncomfortable about the nice things in your house and the food on your table. *Stay home and stay comfortable.*
- Lead someone to the Lord. That is laudable, but it tends to cause excitement and further interest in Christian service. *Proceed with caution.*
- Pull you toward going and serving on other missions again—for the adventure, of course. The problem is that you could slowly, subtly get sucked into thinking about becoming a *missionary.*

and redeemed by Jesus Christ, and therefore is invaluable and worthy of respect as a member of the human family. Every person, from the moment of conception to natural death, has inherent dignity and a right to life consistent with that dignity. Human dignity comes from God, not from any human quality or accomplishment.

Our commitment to the Catholic social mission must be rooted in and strengthened by our spiritual lives. In our relationship with God we experience the conversion of heart that is necessary to truly love one another as God has loved us.[2]

The Seven Key Elements of Catholic Social Teaching Include:

1. LIFE AND DIGNITY OF THE HUMAN PERSON

The Catholic church proclaims that human life is sacred and that the dignity of the human person is the foundation of a moral vision for society. Our belief in the sanctity of human life and the inherent dignity of the human person is the foundation of all the principles of our social teaching. In our society, human life is under direct attack from abortion and assisted suicide. The value of human life is being threatened by increasing use of the death penalty. We believe that every person is precious, that people are more important than things, and that the measure of every institution is whether it threatens or enhances the life and dignity of the human person.

2. CALL TO FAMILY, COMMUNITY AND PARTICIPATION

The person is not only sacred but also social. How we organize our society in economics and politics, in law and policy directly affects human dignity and the capacity of individuals to grow in community. The family is the central social institution that must be supported and strengthened, not undermined. We believe people have a right and a duty to participate in society, seeking together the common good and well-being of all, especially the poor and vulnerable.

3. RIGHTS AND RESPONSIBILITIES

The Catholic tradition teaches that human dignity can be protected and a healthy community can be achieved only if human rights are protected and responsibilities are met. Therefore, every person has a fundamental right to life and a right to those things required for human decency. Corresponding to these rights are duties and responsibilities to one another, to our families, and to the larger society.

4. OPTION FOR THE POOR AND VULNERABLE

A basic moral test is how our most vulnerable members are faring. In a society marred by deepening divisions between rich and poor, our tradition recalls the story of the Last Judgment (Matthew 25:31-46) and instructs us to put the needs of the poor and vulnerable first.

5. THE DIGNITY OF WORK AND THE RIGHTS OF WORKERS

The economy must serve people, not the other way around. Work is more than a way to make a living; it is a form of continuing participation in God's creation. If the dignity of work is to be protected, then the basic rights of workers must be respected: the right to productive work, to decent and fair wages, to organize and join unions, to private property, and to economic initiative.

6. SOLIDARITY

We are our brothers' and sisters' keepers, wherever they live. We are one human family, whatever our national, racial, ethnic, economic and ideological differences. Learning to practice the virtue of solidarity means learning that "loving our neighbor" has global dimensions in an interdependent world.

7. CARE FOR GOD'S CREATION

We show our respect for the Creator by our stewardship of creation. Care for the earth is not just an Earth Day slogan, it is a requirement of our faith. We are called to protect people and the planet, living our faith in relationship with all of God's creation. This environmental challenge has fundamental moral and ethical dimensions that cannot be ignored.[3]

QUESTIONS FOR REFLECTION

1. What challenges do you see today in preserving the dignity of the human person?

2. How do you see your faith-based partnership being able to address those challenges?

3. What are ways we can act to give preferential treatment of the poor, especially in the context of your faith-based partnership?

4. Can you think of any obstacles to a person's dignity of work and rights as a worker? At home? Abroad?

5. What, if any, obstacles exist with people who are involved in your faith-based partnership?

Discovering and "Creating" Solidarity With Faith-based Partners

One summer a few years ago, my daughter traveled with me on a twinning discovery trip to Nicaragua. We were inundated with opportunities to meet people and forge new relationships, but when she and I began to discuss the issue of creating solidarity, her eyes glazed over. "Is it, like, being friends with somebody?" she asked. Yes, but more. "More how?"

We delved deeply into conversation about solidarity, but I don't think I was getting through to her, so we tabled the issue. Then, one afternoon while exploring the grand town square of Granada, Nicaragua, the Holy Spirit descended and provided a lesson in solidarity that "turned the lights on" for us both.

While wandering around the square, visiting a couple of museums and the city's cathedral, we noticed that a girl of maybe ten or eleven began to follow us around, her hands extended hoping for a few coins. At first, my daughter shied away from the girl, worried that she would want to stay with us the rest of our time in Granada. And seeing that the girl was barefoot and dirty, my daughter also was worried about being too close to her, that she might get sick from some germs the girl might have carried.

Instead of giving the girl any alms, I asked her if I could pay her to pose for a couple photographs in the square. I would pay her the equivalent of about a dollar. She agreed, I took the photos and paid her, and the little girl danced away, completely happy.

My daughter was relieved when she left, but I reopened the earlier discussion about solidarity, zeroing in on the commonality of these two young girls despite their cultural and economic differences. "Isn't she a lot like you?" I asked. "She wants to eat, needs ways to make money, feels hunger and pain, and suffers just like we can suffer. Isn't she a young girl, just a little like you?"

I let it go at that, but I think my daughter finally grasped the concept of creating solidarity. Even if only for a moment, my daughter and I accompanied the little girl, albeit briefly, as she traversed her town square.

Margaret Swedish, director of the Religious Task Force on Central America and Mexico, underscores the importance of that "accompaniment" in developing close partnerships, especially when we can walk with our brothers and sisters through repression or persecution and finally understand what it is they face on a daily basis. Creating solidarity requires that we open our eyes and our hearts and then breathe in what it is that our twinning partners are living. Then, Swedish says, we can begin to place ourselves in positions of being able to offer healing, communicating the needs of our partners to folks back home or government leaders, as the need may be. Or, sometimes, it simply is a time when we can reflect on our relationship and offer our prayers for our partners.

A group called Voices on the Border, which has been involved in twinning-type partnerships in Central America for many years, describes something called "active accompaniment," as a cornerstone for solidarity. In its orientation guide, Voices notes that by making the journey to your partner's home, you are:

> Seeing someone else's situation as your own. By experiencing their reality with your own witness, you can better relate and understand the real connections that bind people together… Actively accompanying people in their daily reality allows our solidarity to become not just an abstract idea but to be an integral part of our personal experience, developing a higher level of true understanding of what these people's lives are like and forcing us to reflect on our own.[4]

But creating solidarity goes even beyond the accompaniment. In order to be effective in solidarity, you must ultimately be willing to work on behalf of your sisters and brothers in whatever way you can. Sometimes that means offering prayers, support, money, labor, or other physical attributes. There is another model of solidarity and advocacy that merits consideration, such as the abolitionist movement during the American Civil War era, when anti-slavery leaders not only prayed and walked hand-in-hand with their brothers, they spoke out and sought to change the system that forced those people into bondage.

More recently, in the 1980s, Christian faith communities in North America became involved in the Sanctuary Movement, a loosely consolidated effort to provide havens for Central American refugees seeking political asylum—occurring at a time when the sister-parish movement in the United States was just beginning to take shape.

Today, even as this is being written, faith communities throughout the United States are becoming widely engaged in a discussion about the merits of the Central American Free Trade Agreement (and other similar trade treaties being sought throughout the globe). People of faith, many of them involved in faith-based partnerships with countries that will be greatly affected by these treaties, are engaged in calls to national legislators, asking them to closely examine the efficacy of enacting such "free trade" endeavors. They are asking legislators if it makes sense to put trade relationships in place that promise to displace poor workers, forcing more and more undocumented workers to seek economic asylum in the United States.

Numerous other issues can be cited as core causes in advocacy and solidarity. The labors of solidarity will require commitment, and at some stage, action, by the faith-based partner.

QUESTIONS FOR REFLECTION

1. In your own words, and from your own experiences, define what solidarity really means.

2. Can you site examples of how Christians have engaged in solidarity in order to achieve growth in spirit and faith?

3. How do you envision the issue of solidarity influencing the development of your faith-based partnership?

The Challenges of Poverty

In their document on poverty, "A Place at the Table: A Catholic Recommitment to Overcome Poverty and to Respect the Dignity of All God's Children" the United States Catholic bishops note that three billion poor people earn just over a dollar a day. Add to that figure another three billion people who will be added to developing countries by the year 2050, and you can see there is a tremendous difference between the haves and have-nots in the world. An analysis of further numbers is staggering. According to the document, an estimated 820 million people lack enough food to lead healthy and productive lives, and about 160 million children are seriously underweight for their age.[5]

QUESTIONS FOR REFLECTION

1. Describe illustrations of poverty you have witnessed, either at home or trips away from home; even abroad. What reaction did you have?

2. What can individuals do, indeed, what can you do, to help fight poverty across the globe today?

3. How do you envision your twinning partnership addressing the issue of poverty?

Key Principles in Developing a Positive Faith-based Partnership

There are virtually thousands of ways, big and small, to foster a positive and joyful twinning relationship. The following is a list of those attributes, offered for consideration by twinning leaders in Richmond, Virginia.

Prayer: This is a foundation principle that calls us to build a faith-based partnership around our belief in God. This can involve daily prayer, Bible study, prayer groups, prayer networks, retreats, days of reflection and carefully planned liturgies at Mass, all leading to building positive relationships with twinning partners, one of the most powerful elements of the reciprocity of prayer and experience from the twinning community.

Communication: A crucial element of the partnership involves mutual listening, sharing experiences, understanding each other, patience, and learning new ways to express concerns, joys, faith and social life. Of these tenets of communication, the most important factor for North Americans is listening. We need to open our hearts and minds to the lives of our partners, seeing through their eyes rather than ours. Today we are blessed with numerous ways to stay in touch either via e-mail, telephone, letters, video and audio tapes, photographs, drawings, poems and other creative interactions.

Cultural sensitivity: For better or worse, Americans have a reputation as "my way or the highway" Type-A folks. That is our cultural reality. But as we journey to other lands, especially when we hope to form new relationships with people through twinning partnerships, we need to create an attitude and desire to learn from one another's faith, culture, and daily experiences. Understanding one another's gifts and values actually develops into a responsibility for all people involved in the partnership. The goal, then, is to move to a deeper understanding of our new friends, creating an attitude of mutual equality rather than paternalism and dependency.

Involvement for justice: As we get to know each other, we naturally share our experiences and our lives. When knowledge of injustices surface, one of the most important elements of our relationship is our ability to promote human dignity. That promotion, the raising up of our brothers and sisters, seeking the basic rights to which they are entitled, then becomes an essential element of the relationship. We are called not only to contribute resources to our partners, we also are asked to become actively engaged in the political and social process, using our influence as citizens of perhaps the most powerful country on earth to join the struggle with our faith partners.

Broad-based involvement: When developing a faith-based partnership between twinning partners, it makes sense to involve all facets of the communities that are engaged in the relationship. Thus, a parish in the United States may ultimately want to involve its school in the project. It may ask its social-action committee to become involved in political issues and contact local legislators. Ongoing mutual visits will need to be at the root of the involvement—constant reminders of the partnership.

Closing Prayer

EVANGELIZATION

A Christian community is evangelized in order to evangelize.
A light is lit in order to give light.
A candle is not lit to be put under a bushel, said Christ.
It is lit and put up high in order to give light.

That is what a true community is like.
A community is a group of men and women who have found the truth in Christ and in His Gospel, and who follows the truth and join together to follow it more strongly.

It is not just an individual conversion but a community conversion.
It is a family that believes, a group that accepts God.

In the group, each one finds that the brother or sister is a source of strength and that in moments of weakness they help one another, and by loving one another and believing, they give light.

The preacher no longer needs to preach, for there are Christians who preach by their own lives.

I said once and repeat today that if, unhappily, some day they silence our radio and don't let us write our newspaper, each of you who believe must become a microphone, a radio station, a loudspeaker, not to talk but to call for faith. Amen.[6]

—Archbishop Oscar Romero, from *Living God's Justice: Reflections and Prayers*

NOTES

[1] *Called to Global Solidarity: International Challenges for U.S. Parishes* (Washington, D.C.: USCCB, 1997), p. 1.

[2] "Sharing Catholic Social Teaching: Challenges and Directions," (Washington, D.C.: USCCB, 1999).

[3] Excerpted from *The Seven Key Elements of Catholic Social Teaching* (Washington, D.C.: USCCB, 1999).

[4] From personal handout "El Salvador Delegations: An Orientation Guide" by Voices on the Border. For more information on Voices on the Border visit www.votb.org.

[5] For more information on global poverty read "A Place at the Table: A Catholic Recommitment to Overcome Poverty and to Respect the Dignity of All God's Children" (Washington, D.C.: USCCB, 2002).

[6] *Living God's Justice: Reflections and Prayers* (Cincinnati: St. Anthony Messenger Press, 2006), p. 102.

SECTION II

Preparing for the Journey

New Horizons:
Where You Will Be Traveling

One of the many exciting aspects of being involved in a faith-based partnership is the opportunity to travel and learn about a new place. While that can be learning more about a twinning partner within your state or region, and perhaps even in the more remote corners of the United States, what we will address here is the trip abroad.

By now, your twinning coordinator, delegation leader and perhaps your pastor, have been involved in developing the initial steps required to boarding a plane and actually visiting a faith-based partner or potential twinning partner. Whether you are traveling with a large group sponsored by a diocesan mission office, or statewide synod, or you are part of a small parish team that is breaking new ground in developing a partnership, you will want to learn as much as you can about your twinning partner's country, region or city.

Use the space on the following pages to insert information about your destination country, its people, its history and lessons of faith that will be unique to your hosts.

Gathering information about your faith-based partner's country is easier than ever today, especially with the resources available on the World Wide Web, and detailed information that is available from the United States Government—including the State Department and the Centers for Disease Control and Prevention. Physicians use the CDC Web site (www.cdc.gov) as a primary source of information about the kinds of inoculations that might be necessary for you to safely travel in your destination country.

TRAVEL NOTES:

I will be traveling to ____ .

Dates I will be traveling: ____ .

The culture I will be seeing there is: (Describe culture.)

____

____

____

____

What language do they speak? ____

My level of expertise in that language is: _________________________________

What are some important notes about this country's history, geography and politics that may influence my visit?

List important research resources for learning more about this country:

What have mission societies or missioners you know said about the people and country you will be visiting? What advice do they give?

Other notes about the destination:

Tips for Traveling Abroad

The following travel tips from the United States Department of State come from their Web site at www.state.gov, among other sources.

1. Make sure you have a signed, valid passport and visas, if required. Also, before you go, fill in the emergency information page of your passport.

2. Read the Consular Information Sheets (and public announcements or travel warnings, if applicable) for the countries you plan to visit. Check announcements at www.state.gov/travel.

3. Familiarize yourself with local laws and customs of the countries to which you are traveling. Remember, the United States Constitution does not follow you! While in a foreign country, you are subject to its laws.

4. Make at least two copies of your passport identification page. (I recommend making three or four; leave one copy with your faith community.) This will facilitate replacement if your passport is lost or stolen. Leave one copy at home with friends or relatives. Carry the other with you in a separate place from your passport.

5. Leave a copy of your itinerary with family or friends at home so that you can be contacted in case of an emergency.

6. Do not leave your luggage unattended in public areas. Do not accept packages from strangers.

7. Prior to your departure, you should register with the nearest United States embassy or consulate through the State Department's travel registration Web site. Registration will make your presence and whereabouts known in case it is necessary to contact you in an emergency. *In accordance with the Privacy Act, information on your welfare and whereabouts may not be released without your express authorization. Remember to leave a detailed itinerary and the numbers or copies of your passport or other citizenship documents with a friend or relative in the United States.*

8. To avoid being a target of crime, try not to wear conspicuous clothing and expensive jewelry and do not carry excessive amounts of money or unnecessary credit cards.

9. In order to avoid violating local laws, deal only with authorized agents when you exchange money or purchase art or antiques.

10. If you get into trouble, contact the nearest United States embassy.

11. It helps a great deal to have a United States English-speaking missioner or other reputable person working and waiting for you who knows the local ropes and how to help you on the ground.

Living in a Dangerous World

There's no question that the world is a dangerous place. Even within the United States, we can identify destinations that would require our being constantly on guard. When traveling, it is useful to remember that many of our missionary brothers and sisters have risked—and lost—their lives. According to information collected by Fides News Service, in 2004 fourteen people (priests, religious and lay persons) were killed while engaged in the missionary work of the Catholic church during that calendar year—a figure that flew well under the media's radar screen in the shadow of the war in Iraq, where hundreds were killed.

In 2005 that number grew to twenty five; in 2006, twenty-four priests, nuns or lay workers died in the service of the church.

Africa was the continent that registered the highest number of missionary martyrs—in 2004, four priests, one brother and one sister in the following countries: Burkina Faso, Uganda, Burundi, South Africa, Kenya and Chad.

In the Americas, four priests died violently in 2004, three of them—two in Mexico and one in Guatemala—while working among extreme poverty and degraded social conditions. The fourth, an Italian missionary, was killed in Chile where he had ministered for many years and had grown to love the people; he had even taken Chilean nationality. He was murdered as

Independence Versus Interdependence: Understanding Differences in Cultures

Many North Americans have fully adopted a high-octane, Western lifestyle and often expect everywhere else in the world to respect, if not emulate, our way of living. But one of the great beauties of the twinning experience is discovering that there are other ways of viewing the world. It is useful to compare some of the attributes of culture that we understand compared to what may be found in many other parts of the world. Before departing for your twinning destination, it might prove useful to reflect on a "we versus they" analysis of cultural differences.

Independence versus interdependence: Most North Americans highly respect personal independence, privacy and autonomy, which make up some of the formative constructs of their identity. To be dependent on anyone or anything is considered a weakness and is not desirable. Elsewhere, though, the interdependence one finds within families in The Holy Land's war-torn West Bank or the highlands of Guatemala mark necessary ways of living and surviving. In those societies, Americans often are viewed suspiciously, as people who are out of touch with reality.

Equality versus social hierarchy: The average North American is embarrassed by the demonstrations of deference that highlight inequalities between people; although the opposite is largely

the case, we believe that, in theory, everyone is equal. Elsewhere in the world, however, there is a distinct hierarchy in place that can be found in government, churches and even within families.

Technological orientation versus fatalism: Americans are problem solvers. We believe that if there is a problem, there has to be a way to fix it. We rely heavily on science and technology to provide answers to problems, stating that "where there's a will, there's a way." Travel to other parts of the globe, however, and you will find some people who leave much of their lives to God and fate. "God willing, we will survive this," is at the heart of that philosophy.

Individualism versus solidarity: Science aside, as shown above, North Americans regard themselves as individuals who are competent, self-reliant and assertive. And while North Americans certainly value family, elsewhere in the world the importance of family, as shown earlier, remains a keystone element of life, prompting the virtues of loyalty and solidarity over the needs and desires of the individual.

Tasks versus people: North Americans make liberal use of daily work diaries, electronic organizers, e-mail calendars, cell phones and other devices to get things done. The task, the job, is all-important. Elsewhere you will find that folks are more people-oriented and less job- or task-obsessed.[1]

he left the altar after celebrating Mass for a man said to be a follower of a religious sect. In Brazil, Sister Dorothy Stang paid the ultimate price in January 2005, for providing a voice for the voiceless people of the Amazon rainforest in a confrontation over land-use.

On the continent of Asia, religious fundamentalism contributed to the martyrdom of four people in 2004. Three young Pakistani Catholics were beaten and tortured to death either while under arrest on false charges or in an attempt to make them deny their faith. In India, a priest accused of proselytizing while visiting poor Hindu families, was found brutally murdered.

Violence also occurred within our borders: in 2006, Fides reported that St. Joseph Sister Karen Klimczak was murdered in Buffalo, New York, at the home she had founded for former prisoners.

Thus, when paying a visit to a faith-based partner abroad, it is worth remembering the challenges and dangers that missioners have faced in their line of work.

If you are uncomfortable leaving that safe harbor of home for the sometimes-dangerous waters of the world, you probably should not be making this journey.

Who Are My Traveling Companions?

Imagine the following scenario: You've made the down payment on a luxury hotel at the center of a glorious beach, and have dinner reservations at one of the best five-star restaurants in the country for the evening of your arrival. It promises to be the great start of a trip to remember.

As you open the door to your car, you look inside at the passengers who will accompany you on this grand trip, and all of a sudden it dawns on you: You don't know these people; you barely know their names!

Ever been on a journey like that? Probably not. You certainly don't want that to happen on this twinning immersion trip, either. It's best to know as much as you can about the fellow members of your team *before* you go, so that when you are on the ground in twinning territory, you are able to focus more on what you see and the surroundings and less on the "getting to know you" dance we all go through with people we've just met. Yes, you will make great new friends from your twinning immersion team—that will be an important by-product of the experience overall. But don't lose sight of the real reason for your journey.

There are many ways to accomplish the objective of learning who your fellow travelers are. Here are a few ideas borrowed from groups I've traveled with in the past that seemed to be very effective.

- If your group is large enough (more than ten people), use name tags that are enclosed in clear plastic sleeves and can be pinned to your shirt or jacket. Plan on wearing the name tags for at least the first few days of the trip. It might seem awkward at first, but it serves as an ice-breaker when you are in-country and your hosts can greet you by your first name.

- Ask your team leader/trip coordinator to put together a biography of all travelers. It can be short, sweet and look something like this:

> Dennis O'Connor is making his fifth journey to Guatemala, again writing for *The Catholic Telegraph* newspaper, where he is managing editor. In recent years, Dennis has been joined on immersion trips by his wife of twenty-four years, Paula; his daughter, Colleen; and his son, Sean—all primarily to destinations in Central America. He is a professional photographer, so don't be surprised to see him con-

stantly taking pictures of you, the countryside, and our twinning community. He enjoys golf, reading history and cheering on his children at their school events. Dennis says he hopes to learn more about Guatemalan secondary school programs on this trip.

- Before you leave for your destination, make sure you have a contact list available of all participants that includes names, addresses, home and work phone numbers, and e-mail addresses, at a minimum. There is space at the end of this book for you to staple in such a sheet, or you can use the blank pages in the back of the book to write the information.

- Plan to take a "before" and "after" group photograph that you can paste in this booklet. (And notice the difference in the group dynamics of the before and after poses. Can you see the glow emitting from the *after* photo?)

BEFORE

INSERT PHOTOGRAPH OF YOUR DELEGATION
BEFORE YOUR TRIP HERE.
(Be sure to include a listing, from left to right, of who is in the photo)

- Discover commonalities among the people in your delegation. Teachers can compare notes on how they might apply lessons learned back home in classes, camera buffs can create a plan of attack for ensuring all itinerary items are covered, and linguists can pitch in to help do translating. Think outside of the box: An executive might consider ways to develop business information exchanges with faith partners; a local municipal representative might consider meeting with the mayor of a village; and, if you have a special kind of expertise, share that with your entourage. On a delegation trip to El Salvador a few years ago, one member of our group, an attorney, provided important insights to a woman stranded in-country about immigration issues in the United States.

AFTER

INSERT PHOTOGRAPH OF YOUR DELEGATION
AFTER YOUR TRIP HERE.

Getting Ready: Group Building

Building cohesion within the group that is embarking on a trip to a twinning community is one of the critical first steps to take once you have become part of the "delegation." But just as you wouldn't embark on a weeklong (or longer) journey without planning a detailed itinerary, neither should you depart without having common objectives in place. There are numerous items to do and discuss before departing, such as these ideas offered by Voices on the Border:

- Develop a comprehensive list of what you hope to accomplish on the trip, and discuss what to expect from the group and the twinning community being visited. What do you expect from your group leader? What should your group leader expect from the group? From the outset, the group leader needs to be clear about the objectives of this trip so there is no misunderstanding.

- Share any fears you may have about the trip, including security, visiting a different country or worries about traveling. Discuss ways the group can address your concerns. (Do this early on).

- Share your personal understanding of the social, political and historical situation in your partner's homeland.

- Consider ways for coping with a new culture. Ask what local missionaries might suggest (even better, ask them to make a presentation to your group about the destination based upon their experiences). Plan a daylong retreat to discuss the trip. As often as possible, bring local people from the country to be visited to discuss the destination and its people.

- Share Internet lists and bibliographies of the people/country/community to be visited. One starting point is at the back of this workbook, where numerous Internet resources are listed. Also, *Bridges of Faith* —

the "twinning manual" that accompanies this workbook — contains a lengthy bibliography that will be of interest to all participants.

- Discuss your perceptions of twinning. Is it a relationship based on trust, respect, mutuality, solidarity and shared faith? Are members of the group moving toward a relationship that is defined by partnership, friendship and sharing?

- What can your group do before departure to let others know about your trip? Consider sending out press releases and attempt to discuss the partnership with local media.

- Consider a send-off party and blessing from your faith community.

- Schedule a brainstorming session. Try to come up with creative ways of building your twinning relationship. Invite other faith communities that have engaged in these partnerships and immersion trips to pick their brains as well. Seek the advice of leaders who are actively engaged in the twinning process, such as diocesan or presbytery-level mission coordinators.

- Make pre-delegation commitments to do group and individual follow-up activities such as report-backs, fund-raising events, media interviews, and presentations to civic groups, churches and schools. Do the legwork ahead of time, network as often as possible and harvest the fruits of your labor when you return from your twinning trip.

- Plan in advance how you will preserve the memories of your delegation. Photos, videos and tape recordings can all be used afterwards in multimedia presentations or slide shows. Plan to post information on your Web page, if available.

- Discuss the importance of prayer, daily reflection time, time off, seeing cultural or historical sites, shopping and other time commitments that need to be added to the schedule, and then weigh those against the needs for meetings, visits and travel. Also discuss how much rest members of the group realistically will need in the course of the trip, based on a careful examination of the itinerary. This is particularly important near the end of the trip, when everyone will be tired.

- Discuss the need for having individuals take on specific tasks during the trip: a "round-up" person to get everybody collected together, a water monitor to keep track of drinking water, a designated translator—if needed—to help when delegation leader is occupied, an official photographer, and other duties that might be recurrent on your trip.

- Begin to formulate a mission statement that can be mutually agreed upon with the twinning partner. Two examples of mission statements and covenants between faith-based partners can be found in the appendix of *Bridges of Faith*.[2]

Ten Commandments for Twinning Trip Participants

1. Don't expect to find things as you would find them at home. After all, you've left home to experience a different world.

2. Don't take anything too seriously. A willingness to accept things as they are lays the foundation for a good trip to another country. Be flexible and adaptable, and have a sense of humor.

3. Don't let other group members get on your nerves. You have gone to great pains to make this journey.

4. Don't forget that you represent your country, your church and Jesus Christ on this trip.

5. Don't worry too much about the destination. Too much worry will take away from the positive potentials of the trip. Few things people worry about are ever fatal.

6. Never, ever lose your passport.

7. Remember the advice "When in Rome, do as the Romans do." When in doubt, try to use your good common sense.

8. Do not judge an entire people by the trouble you may have had with one of their members.

9. Remember that you are a guest; treat your host with respect, and you will be treated as an *honored* guest.

10. Enjoy yourself and savor the moments. Even if you never are able to return to your faith-partner's country, you'll always remember the time you were able to make the visit.[3]

What to Bring

There is a time-worn saying that travelers should pack their bags, step back and then take a deep breath. Once relaxed, remove half of what is packed, and then bring twice as much money as originally planned.

While that approach sounds simplistic and a little cynical, there's a bit of truth to the axiom about over-packing. Always surrounded by our "stuff," North Americans love to have the important things in life along on a trip. But it's important to keep several things in mind. First, this isn't a vacation. This is very much a pilgrimage, one in which the prudent participant will remember he or she needs to be rooted in practicality and—let's hope—appropriate levels of humility. Go as a "student" to learn and appreciate others in different cultures. Since it is likely you will be traveling to a destination where the standard of living is below yours, you may want to be conservative and modest with the clothing and accessories you decide to bring. Leave the diamond-studded watch at home; instead, bring along a twenty-dollar timepiece.

But having said that, you also must keep in mind no matter where you are headed you will be away from home, and it is important to bring along clothing and other items that you will need. Different destinations, different climates and customs, indeed, different cultural situations will ultimately dictate many of the decisions you will make as you pack. The list on p. 36 is not meant to be completely comprehensive, but it will serve as one set of suggested "basics" you will want to consider for your journey. At the end of the suggested list is space for you to add items that your group has determined are necessary for the destination in question.

DOCUMENTATION

You'll know it's not a dream any more when you hear the words "May I see your passport, please?"

Passport, driver's license, possibly a church identification card and other forms of ID all are items you will need. Many travelers find it useful to bring along an internationally recognized driver's license. You also will want to have copies of all the important documents, especially your airline ticket and passport, in the event any of the original items disappear. If necessary, you also should bring an International Certificate of Vaccination (ask your delegation leader or travel agent; they'll know if you need it or not).

Many delegation leaders suggest making up photocopy packets of information that contain copies of your passport (including the cover, inside pages where your photo is posted, and any visas attached), copies of your airline ticket (or, if traveling ticketless, the airline confirmation number and flight itinerary), copies of your air and ground itinerary, where you will be staying (listing addresses, phone numbers, confirmation numbers for booking purposes and Web site addresses), and all emergency contact information you can get beforehand.

Also in this packet can be emergency medical information, eyeglass or medical prescription data, and related information. You should keep one copy with your suitcases, give one copy to your family, and provide at least one copy to somebody at your church or faith community. Also useful for folks back home is a comprehensive list of all telephone numbers (in-country airline numbers, United States embassy telephone numbers, cell phone numbers of hosts, and any others that might be available to you in advance of departure). The idea, quite simply, is to leave no stone unturned when it comes to any kind of emergency, whether that is a misplaced airline ticket or a healthcare problem.

BOOKS, MAPS, CAMERAS AND FILM

A writer by trade, I always bring a map of the country, region and city I will be traveling through. Every time I travel, I have occasion to pull out the map and ask locals where we are at a given moment, or I've asked someone to show me how we will get to a particular destination. When traveling to urban destinations, city maps also can be helpful. While navigating the hazardous traffic in Managua, Nicaragua, with a Jesuit priest some years ago, having a city map handy would later help me retrace that day's adventures in my journal that evening. I write freely on these maps, circling interesting sights and writing brief notes in the margins describing topography, an unusual geographic feature, where a sweatshop was in relationship to the international airport, and so on. When back home, I often pull out travel maps to help describe the journey, showing where we went, circling the parameters of the trip on the ground and demonstrating how difficult it was driving along muddy roads through a memorable mountain pass, or where our bus was halted by a herd of cattle. Most major bookstores have fairly comprehensive map sections, and you can locate maps for virtually any destination on the Internet with a Google or Yahoo search.

I also try to bring travel books along about the destinations. While books such as *Bridges of Faith* offer an in-depth analysis of the hows and whys of faith-based partnerships, it is always handy to have a book that provides information about the local currency, listings of banks that will cash travelers checks, telephone numbers to the major airlines in-country, the most interesting tourist destinations in a given region, hospital and health-care information, and so on. Invariably, members of your delegation will appreciate the "expert" information that you've helped provide.

Often, leaders of twinning immersion trips will ask other team members to bring along specific kinds of books, maps or other information to be shared by the group. One member might bring along a United States State Department country book about Honduras, while another member might bring a couple books about the ancient Mayan site of Copan—scene of a half-day trip that might be scheduled into the itinerary of a twinning trip to Honduras, as only one example. You also may want to bring a novel about the culture you are visiting to help put your experiences into context.

Finally, there is the question of cameras. Digital cameras are relatively inexpensive these days and offer plenty of data-storage options. Because of increased airport security (and endless opportunities to have your film "burned" via X-ray machines), digital cameras are the way to go for most travelers now.

Should you consider bringing a video camera? That is a question only you can answer. But you should consider the expense of the camera should it be lost, damaged or stolen: Will your insurance cover it on this trip? And you also should consider the bulkiness of the video camera, even a very small one, as you are bused around country or have to hike to remote stretches of your partner's turf. Conversely, the benefit of having video of the trip is tremendous: Someone with editing equipment can produce a first-class documentary of the experience, making the telling of stories that much easier and perhaps a bit better than a good laptop computer presentation created from your digital still photographs.

MEDICINE AND FIRST-AID KITS

The well-prepared delegation leader will have on hand a fairly comprehensive first-aid kit for the entire group. These are the $150-$200 first-aid kits you can buy from outdoor outfitters and online at survival Web sites. But every traveler should have at least a basic first-aid kit containing a wide variety of sterile bandages, ointments, aspirin, eye drops, alcohol wipes and so on. A trip to the local drug store will net an adequate personal first-aid kit for less than twenty dollars.

Add to that kit items such as anti-diarrhea pills, over-the-counter treatments for sinus infections, as well as any physician-prescribed medication you need to bring along. If you have a prescription that you need to bring, consider having your doctor write a prescription for double that amount, in case anything is lost or damaged during the trip. Always bring prescription drugs in the original container issued at your pharmacy. When possible, ask for generic prescriptions, which will be easier to fill in an emergency on the road.

A tip from Archie Bruun, a longtime mission coordinator for the Catholic church and a native of Bolivia, advises travelers to always describe the prescription items as "medicine," and not "drugs," thus alleviating any misunderstanding at the customs desk when entering your twinning partner's country.

And finally, the ultimate antibacterial medicine: Cipro. Always check with a physician in advance and discuss where you are traveling. Your doctor will be able to offer the best advice concerning what kinds of medication you should bring along as a matter of course. However, you will find when discussing such trips with acquaintances that the most frequently mentioned drug is Cipro, a broad-based medicine that is available by prescription only.

One final note on health: While considering medicines for travel, it also is advisable to peruse the United States Government's health advisories for the country and region you will be traveling. Recommended inoculations and precautions will be listed at the Centers for Disease Control and Prevention's Web site: www.cdc.gov.

Clothing and Accessories

The following is a basic checklist that can be supplemented with other items your delegation leader or twinning partner might recommend to bring along as well. Carry-on baggage should contain essential documents such as your passport and airline tickets, as well as prescription medicines and one change of clothing. Along with your passport, store any credit cards, travelers' checks and cash safely on your person. A money belt is a must for holding important items when traveling overseas.

The items below can all be packed in your check-in luggage. Scratch off items you know you won't need:

- ❑ Address book
- ❑ Bible
- ❑ Bed sheet/blanket/pillowcase or other sleeping gear
- ❑ Backpack/haversack
- ❑ Bathing suit
- ❑ Batteries for flashlight, tape player, etc.
- ❑ Calculator
- ❑ Camera
- ❑ Clothes hangers
- ❑ Clothesline & clothes pins
- ❑ Duct tape (small roll)
- ❑ Earplugs
- ❑ English/foreign language dictionary if traveling to non-English speaking country
- ❑ Eyeglasses (and a spare pair)/extra contact lenses and cleaning solution
- ❑ Foot powder
- ❑ Flashlight
- ❑ Gifts for hosts (small, inexpensive)
- ❑ Gym shoes, walking shoes and sandals (extra shoelaces)
- ❑ Hand sanitizer
- ❑ Hat/cap
- ❑ Insect repellent (with DEET)
- ❑ Journal, and a small notebook for taking notes
- ❑ Laundry soap (small liquid packets stored in a plastic bag)
- ❑ Light jacket (heavier if weather dictates)
- ❑ Pants/skirts
- ❑ Pens and pencils
- ❑ Photos of family members, fellow parishioners
- ❑ Plastic garbage bags (for soiled laundry)
- ❑ Raincoat or poncho
- ❑ Resealable sandwich bags, large
- ❑ Sandals
- ❑ Sewing kit
- ❑ Shirts
- ❑ Socks

❏ Sunscreen
❏ Sunglasses
❏ Sweater/sweatshirt
❏ Tape player and tapes or MP3 player or other listening/recording devise
❏ Thank you cards
❏ Toiletries (razor, shampoo, toothpaste, toothbrush)
❏ Toilet paper or small packs of tissues
❏ T-shirts
❏ Travel alarm clock
❏ Underwear
❏ Umbrella
❏ Walking shorts
❏ Washcloth and towel
❏ Water bottle
❏ Wet wipes

Other items not on the list above:

❏ ______________________________

❏ ______________________________

❏ ______________________________

❏ ______________________________

❏ ______________________________

❏ ______________________________

❏ ______________________________

❏ ______________________________

❏ ______________________________

❏ ______________________________

❏ ______________________________

Tips for Journaling

One of the most important aspects of your journey in building bridges of faith is telling the stories about what you have seen, touched, heard, tasted, smelled, thought and smiled about.

The rare few of us who possess photographic memories can recall everything they've done on a given day, but most of us rely on notes, diaries or journals to allow us to revisit memorable events. Because of the importance of the trip you are taking, and since storytelling and retelling (and writing articles or scripts for presentations, etc.) will rely on accurate recollections of your journey, the most efficient tool you have is your journal or diary.

Here are some tips for effective journaling that may be useful.

- Use *Bridges of Faith* as part of your journaling mechanism, posting important permanent data in this workbook as reference for your journal writing. Key addresses, group photographs, maps and itineraries can all be stapled within the book for permanent record-keeping.

- Obtain a new blank journal for your trip. A good, hardcover journal can be found at most bookstores and is well worth the investment. Your journal is something that should be able to weather your trip and many years on your bookshelf at home. The journal should be for this trip only. Pages not used for journal entries can hold additional photographs, ticket stubs, flyers and other items from your trip.

- Always carry a small notepad in your pocket to jot down notes, names, quick observations, phone numbers, comments made, and other information that can be posted in your journal later in the day. Meanwhile, your journal should be stored in a safe place such as your suitcase.

- Set aside quiet time every day to write in your journal. Keep your itinerary handy to refer to the list of events that were scheduled, and try to write at minimum a line or two about each scheduled event.

- Pledge to write as much as you can every day. Remember, you may not come this way again, so you want to ensure you can describe what you saw. This doesn't have to be the Great American Novel, just a series of notes that you can use to trigger memories about your trip. Make the entries while the experiences are fresh in your mind.

- Record your observations of the day. Recall the weather, the temperature, road conditions. Were crops near harvest? How were the people dressed? How did this contrast with what you see at home? How were the people just like everyone back home? How were they different?

- One of the many questions you'll get when you are back home is "What was the food like?" Describe your memorable meals, good or bad. If possible, bring a recipe or two home with you. What are the markets like? Are there shopping centers like at home? Street markets? Street vendors?

- Try to recall at least one conversation from the day. It can be a short, descriptive paragraph about the content of the conversation or something akin to an abridged version of the whole event. Conversations later can be made into quotes that you will use in your storytelling endeavors.

- Ask yourself what your emotions were at the end of the day. What moved you most? What changed you most, and why?

- Don't be afraid to compare notes with fellow travelers. If a recollection seems cloudy, ask them now; if you wait until you all are home, you may lose the opportunity to bring that image to light.

- Consider reserving space in your journal (maybe toward the back of the book) where your host(s) can sign your book and perhaps write a line or two (ala your high-school yearbook).

Five Tips for Safe Travel in Foreign Lands

OK, you are almost ready to go. The excitement of traveling to new places may tempt you to let down your guard. Then you become easy prey for thieves or worse. As you prepare to hit the road on that immersion trip, impress these final safe travel tips in your memory:

- Keep your luggage nearby and within your view. If traveling by air, check your baggage in as soon as you arrive at the airport. Only allow airline personnel and uniformed skycaps to handle your baggage.

- Don't flash cash in public. When buying something at a store, don't pull out a huge wad of money (even if it seems like "play" money to you). When you travel, wear a money belt or sack under your clothes to carry your cash and small valuables. Don't leave valuables in a car or hotel room when you're not there.

- Keep your address somewhat private. If you're staying in a hotel, don't disclose your room number when strangers are within earshot. Be reluctant about opening your door for unexpected visitors or deliveries without calling the front desk to verify the visitor's identity.

- Be alert for deliberate mishaps. Thieves and pickpockets distract people with ploys like bumping into someone or spilling a drink on people in a crowd.

- Keep hotel room doors and windows locked. Don't leave a hotel room door ajar while you go down the hall for an errand. If you find your room door open after you had left it closed, return to the hotel lobby and ask that someone go with you back to the room.[4]

NOTES

[1] Adapted from Louise Fiber Luce and Elise C. Smith, eds. *Toward Internationalism: Readings in Cross-Cultural Communication* (Cambridge, Mass.: Newbury House, 1987).

[2] Adapted from "El Salvador Delegations: An Orientation Guide" by Voices on the Border.

[3] Howard Culbertson, "Ten Commandments for Mission Trip Participants." Available at www.ShortTermMissions.com.

[4] Howard Culbertson, "Five Tips for Safe Travel." Available at www.ShortTermMissions.com.

SECTION III

When You Arrive

Understanding the Process of the Trip "On the Ground"

The well-organized immersion trip is a thing of beauty: An itinerary has been drawn up that accurately reflects what might be expected during the day-to-day of your journey. Travel arrangements have all been coordinated, lunches have been packed and dinner is all arranged. A guest speaker will greet the group at the first stop; in the afternoon, you'll see firsthand how coffee is harvested. That's the way we like things in America: Everything happens like clockwork, and when it doesn't, it can be quickly fixed.

But on this trip, things may be different. On any given day, you may have an experience in which everything goes haywire. The speaker is late. Lunch never arrives. The bus gets stuck in a muddy rut on the way up a hill. And the coffee workers have asked to reschedule to another day because there is a strike.

Sometimes although you expect to operate on a tight schedule and get a lot done during the day, your hosts may be more relaxed or, at times, unable to deliver on requested itinerary items.

Sit back, relax and soak up the ambience of what life is like in this new world, a place unfamiliar and about as distant from home as can be. Thus, when the interpreter fails to show up for your day trip to the capital city, use this as a chance to brush up on your language skills. A delayed speaker or dignitary sets the stage for an animated discussion about the history of a village perched over a beautiful farming valley. A broken-down bus can translate into a wonderful photo opportunity, and perhaps a delightful stroll to the hamlet around the bend ahead, where surprised villagers offer smiles and hospitality.

During one twinning immersion trip I participated in a few years ago, I was part of a group going by boat via the widest stretch of Lake Atitlan in Guatemala to a hotel where we would stop for a one-day break from a frenetic week of travel. Just more than halfway across the lake, our boat's motor ran out of gas. We laughed nervously; someone offered to hop out and "swim" the boat to the opposite shore—an improbable task even for the best swimmer. But after a while, we all were lulled into silence, the boat rocking lightly back and forth, and we looked at the stars and listened to the wind blowing ever so gently over the water. Not quite thirty minutes later, we were rescued and were checked into our hotel. But at dinner that night, we all marveled at the experience of being adrift, like the ancients who had plied the waters of that lake for a thousand years, in the shadows of two volcanoes, somewhere in a time and distance so very far away from home.

Thus, the unscheduled events often provide the most vivid and cherished memories of your journey.

Your Faith-based Partners

You will be able to provide detailed insights about your twinning partners in your journal, but consider using the space below to record the basics about your faith-based partners. This questionnaire, developed by Ren Austing, twinning coordinator at St. James of the Valley Parish in Wyoming, Ohio, is an excellent survey of the faith partners. While some of the questions are geared to ongoing relationships, the queries help provide a broad illustration of your twinning companions. It should be done in-country during your visit.

ABOUT THE FAITH-BASED PARTNERSHIP

Who are our faith-based partners? What is the name of their community and their church?

Who are the key contacts among our faith partners? What are their addresses, e-mail addresses and phone numbers?

What are the dreams and desires of our faith-based partners? What are the important dimensions of life they have shown me during this immersion trip?

How does the twinning relationship impact their community? What do you see as the greatest benefits, and the greatest challenges in the relationship?

What does solidarity mean to the community? How does (will) the partnership reflect this definition? How could the relationship better reflect solidarity in the future?

ABOUT THE COMMUNITY

What are the most significant challenges to the community?

What are the most significant strengths of the community?

THE REALITY OF THE INDIVIDUAL

What are the most significant opportunities and challenges to individual community members and their families?

What is the economic reality of the individuals?

What are the predominant occupations of the community members?

What are typical wages/benefits of these occupations?

Do these typical wages provide sufficiently for the needs of the workers and their families? Specifically, do these wages provide for items recognized as necessities under Catholic social teaching (are these "living" wages)?

What would be the annual wages an individual would need to make in this community to provide a decent living for his or her family?

What are the levels of unemployment and underemployment in the community? What are the causes of unemployment here?

Are there any connections between the employers of community members and international trade?

What members of the typical family work outside the home?

SYSTEMIC ISSUES AND INTERNATIONAL, ECONOMIC AND POLITICAL INTERRELATEDNESS

What are the most serious domestic systemic (governmental, economic, cultural) obstructions to the well-being of the community and the individuals?

How do international, political and economic policies impact the lives of community members? What are the greatest benefits and challenges of these connections?

What opinions do community members take on free trade treaties?

What advocacy issues would be of most importance to the community and individuals for North Americans to learn about and work on?

A Note on Sharing Gifts

Gift-giving is a common practice among people involved in faith-based partnerships. Whether gifts of small items that serve as mementos of your home or handmade items that will remind you of your twinning partners, gifts given in a faithful exchange are wonderful gestures.

But gifts can get out of hand, and too often we misunderstand the nature of the exchange of gift-giving.

What is a gift? In Pakisa K. Tshimika and Tim Lind's book, *Sharing Gifts in the Global Family of Faith*, it is broken down to its simplest level:

> First, a gift is something that is *given*; it is something that moves from one person to another. Second, a gift is something given *voluntarily*. It cannot be forced or required. And third, a gift is something given voluntarily *without regard to compensation*. It is different from something being sold or exchanged, where we expect equivalent value in return for what we give.[1]

Tshimika and Lind further explain that there is a complete freedom involved in gift-giving, in which the gift is released with no strings attached to the person receiving the gift. A gift is a smile. A gift is a handshake, a prayer, a Poloroid photo, a pencil and eraser. Even deeper, they note, gifts given to us—our talents, our time, sometimes our money—are meant to be shared with others.

Thus the very experience of gift-giving in many ways goes to the very heart of our faith-based partnership.

There is a danger, though, with gift-giving. North Americans, especially, are pegged as a class of people who often attach strings to "gifts." When offering money, there is a temptation to make demands on how it is used. That flows from the practice of our government, which has a history of being generous with grants to developing nations, so long as certain benchmarks are met by the recipient. We find it easy to follow suit.

Perhaps the best way to view gift-giving is to frame the process in terms of friendship. You want to make new friends, but you don't go over to your friend's home and tell them that everything in their house is wrong, and then to help out you begin the process of remaking the house for them in a manner you think it should be done. Who needs friends like that?

The following is an excerpt from the study guide for *Sharing Gifts in the Global Family of Faith* that takes an initial survey of gift-giving within a faith community.[2]

THINKING ABOUT GIFTS

1. Make a list of all the persons to whom you give gifts. How do the gifts you give affect your relationship with the recipient? Who do you receive gifts from? How do the gifts you receive affect your relationship with the donor?

2. Number the following motives for giving in the order in which they primarily motivate our giving:

   – Being nice.
   – It's expected.
   – I'd like to get something back.
   – I get more satisfaction from giving than keeping.
   – I can't help it.
   – I want to do everything I can for our common good.

3. When you give, do you feel that your resources have been enlarged or reduced?

4. Tell about a gift you've received—or given—that has built or extended a relationship.

5. Tell about a gift you've received—or given—that did little to nourish a relationship.

6. How might our gift-giving change if we firmly believed that its primary purpose is to connect us with each other and to nourish relationships?

7. Are some gifts superior to others? How do you decide?

8. Who *should be* the beneficiaries of your congregation's gifts?

9. Who *are* the beneficiaries?

The Keys to a Quality Debriefing*

A quality debriefing experience—a detailed discussion of what occurred on the immersion trip—is one key that unlocks the potential of long-term life change for most delegation members. As a delegation leader, planning and executing the debriefing sessions is like putting the key in the lock. It is up to the delegation members to "turn the key" as they engage in the process with you and open their hearts. Here are several principles that will help prepare for a quality debriefing experience for all parties.

1. *Make it a priority from the start.* You can't wait until your trip is over, bags are packed, and the delegation is standing in the airport waiting for the flight number to be called to think about debriefing and expect it to be productive. Decide in advance that you are going to gather at a designated time to process the whirlwind of events and activities you have experienced together. Everyone should be in agreement as to the time, place and duration of the meeting.

2. *Plan to hold debriefing sessions in your host country.* Most twinning team members have an internal switch that goes off as soon as your plane touches the ground back home (for some it's just being in our airspace that does it!). Team members tend to become preoccupied, focused on reconnecting with their friends, family members and favorite fast-food meal upon returning home. There is a measure of honesty, vulnerability and team chemistry that is nearly impossible to recreate outside of your host country. There also may be questions to address that can best be answered by the host representative.

3. *Schedule interim debriefing sessions on a daily basis.* A grueling schedule will limit the time you can dedicate to a daily gathering—put together as a time for prayer and reflection—but it is a way to cap the day and help set priorities for the group at the end of the trip. Promise to revisit items at the end of the trip if they cannot all be addressed at once.

4. *Emphasize the importance of debriefing throughout the trip.* Keep track of events, ideas, opportunities, and challenges that you want to address with the group before you leave.

5. *Select the location for your debriefing sessions carefully.* Often in-country contacts suggest you combine a visit to a tourist area with the debriefing sessions. If this seems to be the best use of time, make sure you go to a secluded area away from potential distractions to hold your debriefing sessions. Be sure to instruct your team members in advance that priority one is debriefing and priority two free time at the tourist site.

6. *Be realistic with your time allotment.* Quality debriefing sessions cannot be rushed. This is the one time in the trip that everyone must agree to sit down and listen to everyone as they have an opportunity to express their opinions and thoughts about the journey.

7. *Emphasize the priority issues.* Take a good look at the big picture. Try to examine the important aspects that your faith-based partner has brought to the table. Ask how you can most fully participate in their lives.

8. *Be ready to strike while the iron is hot.* You will be most energized about your experience when you have just returned from your trip. Be prepared to brief your faith community at home about the experience. Be committed to the long-term plan of telling the story after you have returned.[3]

* This section is specifically addressed to the delegation leader.

NOTES

[1] Pakisa K. Tshimkia and Tim Lind. *Sharing Gifts in the Global Family of Faith: One Church's Experience* (Intercourse, Penn.: Good Books, 2003), p. 25.

[2] Excerpted from Pakisa K. Tshimkia and Tim Lind. *Study Guide to Sharing Gifts in the Global Family of Faith: One Church's Experience* (Intercourse, Penn.: Good Books, 2003).

[3] Steve Moore, "Keys to a Quality Debriefing." Available at www.ShortTermMission.com.

SECTION IV

Returning Home

Returning Home: Steps to a Successful After-Trip Program

Reverend Joe Bragotti, a Comboni missioner who has logged many years in Latin America and Africa, understands the challenges people face when they have returned from a short-term immersion trip.

"When you stay away from home for a long time, we often say that you never really can return home, because in the interim, you and home have both changed."

While that is not necessarily true of a brief encounter of a week or two, certainly you will have discovered you've changed, and you will find yourself in a position in which you want to effect change on those around you, your parish and your family and friends.

Bragotti, who was a co-founder of the group Mission to Mission, has been involved in programs that helped reintroduce missionaries to their home countries after returning from relatively short to nearly lifelong absences from their homes.

"Sometimes we have to develop new skills," he says. "The idea is to treasure your experiences and then turn that experience into a useful ministry back home." The same is true of those involved in twinning partnerships. He notes that while Mission to Mission has had great success working with missioners on their adjustments home, "we didn't want to create a situation where we had somebody a hundred percent reintegrated into the home environment. We wanted to maintain some of the edge they developed while overseas."

He suggests several steps for making the adjustment back home after taking an immersion trip, including:

- Review the trip thoroughly. A good debriefing as a group, done before departing the country being visited, is a productive way to cover all the bases of the trip. Remember what you did with the group, what discoveries individuals may have made on their own. Be realistic about the experience: There may have been good points and bad points, but all the experiences provide lessons for the group.

- Internalize the experience. What were the positives and what were the negatives from the trip? Were the negatives avoidable, or were they intrinsic to the experience?

- Make peace with the negatives of the trip.

- Ask yourself, "What did this mean to me? How did I change? What impact did the trip have on my life? On the lives of those I visited?"

- Decide what you are going to do with this experience. Tell the story and give the basic idea behind the story: Why did we do this trip? Why did people act the way they did?

- If you are able to publicize the experience well within the faith community back home, there is the beginning of a chance for advocacy on behalf of your new faith-partners. Ask yourself what can be done now to affect the issues of poverty, unemployment, and other problems that our brothers and sisters face?

- The crowning glory of the whole experience is becoming aware of international issues through the twinning process, where we discover why people are poor, why certain conflicts exist, and where we fit in the bigger scheme of things.

- Decide how to remember and share your stories. Take full advantage of the Internet, and post stories and photos on a Web site dedicated to the partnership. Think in advance about creating tools that can be used to retell the story: videos, photo albums, written testimonies, scheduled discussions and lectures. Take every available opportunity to tell the stories that you have gathered.

- Consider the mechanisms that might be used to stay in touch with the community that was your host. E-mail, letters, and even occasional telephone calls can be exchanged to update both faith communities about what is new, what needs have arisen or what prayers might be shared. Be aware that at some point, your faith-based partner(s) may someday ask you for help or money to get into the United States—often a daunting task.

- Invite the twinning partners to visit us back home. Identify who might be able to come, when and how long they might stay, and how the mechanics of such a visit can be carried out. Be aware, however, that getting into the United States has become very difficult, posing one of the greatest challenges to the faith-based partnerships today. This will be an area where help from other experienced faith communities may be able to provide counsel, especially when dealing with a specific country.

- Advocate on behalf of your twinning friends. This can be anything from contacting legislators about particular international trade agreements to specific requests for help on development projects in their communities.

- Reflect on how have you changed and what have you gained.

- Developing long-term networking with other twinning parishes and your home mission office.

- Consider the importance of group reunions and reflections.

- Decide whether lay mission work is possible for you. Seek advice from a spiritual director or local mission office.

- See if there are ways to impact your school, parish and community with your twinning experience. (Note: Several publications dealing with the process of returning home for missioners and twinning delegations are available from Mission to Mission and can be ordered from their web site: www.missiontomission.org.)

Building Bridges With Your Web Site

Clearly one of the greatest communications tools now available to faith communities for spreading the word about twinning partnerships is the World Wide Web. Whether sharing a page on an existing church Web site or developing a new Web site for the partnership, several elements might be considered for inclusion:

- Accounts of delegation trips to the twinning partners' home, including articles from delegation members, photographs of the trip and photos of people from the twinning faith community.

- Information on how people within the parish can become involved in the twinning process, along with contacts and phone numbers.

- Links to other sites that might include diocesan mission office, and groups such as Catholic Relief Services, Mission to Mission, Maryknoll and others.

- If available, consider linking to other parishes or churches in the diocese or nearby, including contact information.

Resources

One of the most effective means of telling the story of your twinning immersion trip is to have some kind of press coverage about the trip and the group. To the right is a sample press release that can be sent to local newspapers, radio and television stations for them to consider doing a story on your journey.

A SAMPLE PRESS RELEASE

FOR IMMEDIATE RELEASE
Contact information:
E-mail address:
Web site information:

Local Parishioners Return From Twinning Trip in Africa
ANYWHERE, USA—Members of St. Anthony of Padua Parish in Little Springs recently returned from a two-week trip in San Salvador, El Salvador, where they met with their "sister parish" partners at St. Joseph Church in the inner city of the capital. According to Reverend Joe Johnston, who led the group of about a dozen parishioners from Little Springs, the delegation's trip was the culmination of two year's planning, when the concept of "faith-based partnerships" was introduced to the North Americans.

"It was a trip of a lifetime for many of the folks from our parish," Johnston said. "We were witness to extremes of poverty, yet at the same time, we also were able to see the deep faith and hospitality of the people of St. Joseph Church and how welcoming they were to us."

(Add comments from perhaps three to four additional persons in the party, and try to end the press release on one sheet.)

Interviews are available with Reverend Johnston and other members of the St. Anthony of Padua Parish.

Photos enclosed

Complete press packet from the trip available on our Web site, noted above.

HELPFUL WEB SITES

The following Internet resources might be useful in preparing for and fostering ongoing faith-based partnerships.

JUSTICE AND PEACE CONCERNS

Maryknoll Office for Global Concerns—Peace, social justice and integrity of creation in Africa, Asia, Latin America and the Middle East.
See http://www.maryknoll.org/
    GLOBAL/OFFICE/linklist.htm.

Documents relating to Catholic social justice teaching—Statements relating to social justice by popes, church councils, national bishops' conferences, and individual bishops.
See http://www.justpeace.org/docu.htm.

Parish without Borders—Using the Internet to interconnect the resources and needs of Catholics in the United States with Catholic communities in Africa, Asia and Latin America in the full spirit of Gospel teaching.
See http://parish-without-borders.net.

Woodstock Theological Center—An independent research institute that addresses topics of social, economic, and political importance from a theological and ethical perspective.
See http://georgetown.edu/centers/
    woodstock.

NETWORK—A national Catholic social justice lobby.
See http://www.igc.org/network.

Macronet—A nonprofit clearinghouse for progressives emphasizing peace, justice, environmental, and health issues and solutions.
See http://www.macronet.org/macronet.

Office of Social Development and World Peace—Part of the United States Catholic Conference, works on issues of landmines, children, Third World debt, the Middle East, death penalty and food policy.
See http://www.usccb.org/sdwp.

Campaign for Human Development—The domestic anti-poverty social justice program of the United States Catholic bishops.
See http://www.usccb.org/cchd.

Volunteer Missionary Movement—Founded in 1969 by Edwina Gately. More than one thousand women and men have worked in Africa, Papua New Guinea, Central America and the United States. It remains the only independent, lay, international mission organization rooted in the Catholic tradition.
See http://vmmusa.org.

Pax Christi, U.S.A.—A Catholic peace movement for prayer, study, and action.
See http://www.paxchristiusa.org.

Witness for Peace—A faith-based organization dedicated to nonviolence, focusing on United States involvement in Latin America and the Caribbean.
See http://witnessforpeace.org.

S.O.A. Watch—A group that monitors the United States Army School of the Americas operated in Ft. Benning, Georgia.
See http://www.soaw.org.

Project Ploughshares—The Institute of Peace and Conflict Studies at Waterloo, Canada.
See http://www.ploughshares.ca.

ECONOMIC JUSTICE

Ten Thousand Villages—Stores that provide vital, fair income to Third World artisans by marketing their handicrafts and telling their stories in North America.
See http://www.tenthousandvillages.com.

Equal Exchange—Fair trade coffee retailers. Site includes information about interfaith coffee program.
See http://equalexchange.com.

Global Exchange—A nonprofit research, education, and action center dedicated to promoting people-to-people ties around the world. Works on fair trade, world bank and International Monetary Fund, speaker tours, and other economic alternatives.
See http://www.globalexchange.org.

National Labor Committee—Reports, educational resources and action items on working conditions worldwide.
See http://www.nlcnet.org.

OTHER RESOURCES ON THE INTERNET

American Friends Service Committee
http://www.afsc.org

Bread for the World
http://www.bread.org

Catholic Institute for International Relations
http://www.ciir.org

Center for Global Education at Augsburg College
http://www.augsburg.edu/global

Center for International Policy
http://www.ciponline.org

CISPES (concentrating on El Salvador)
http://cispes.org

Cooperative for Education (Guatemala)
http://www.coeduc.org

Fahamu Networks for Social Justice (Africa)
http://www.fahamu.org

Fellowship of Reconciliation: Task Force on Latin America
and the Caribbean
http://www.forusa.org

Friends Committee on National Legislation
http://www.fcnl.org

Guatemala Human Rights Commission
http://www.ghrc-use.org

Institute for Policy Studies
http://www.ips-dc.org

International Labor Rights Fund
http://www.laborrights.org

Jesuit Refugee Service/USA
http://www.jesuit.org/JCOSIM/jrs

Lawyers Committee for Human Rights
http://www.lchr.org

Mennonite Central Committee
http://www.mcc.org

Mexico Solidarity Network
http://www.mexicosolidarity.org

Minnesota Advocates for Human Rights
http://mnadvocates.org

NETWORK, A national Catholic social justice lobby
http://www.networklobby.org

Nicaragua Network
http://www.nicanet.org

NISGUA, Network in Solidarity with the People of
Guatemala
http://www.nisgua.org

North American Congress on Latin American
http://www.nacla.org

Oxfam America
http://www.oxfam.org

Peace Brigades International
http://www.peacebrigades.org

Religious Task Force on Central America
http://www.rtfcam.org

SHARE Foundation (El Salvador)
http://www.share-elsalvador.org

United States Catholic Conference
http://www.usccb.org

Voices on the Border (El Salvador)
http://www.votb.org

Washington Office on Latin America
http://www.wola.org

Witness for Peace
http://witnessforpeace.org

Index

EXTRA JOURNAL SPACE